SHORT WALKS
MADE EASY

FOREST
BOWLAND

Ordnance Survey

Contents

Getting outside in the Forest of Bowland 6

We smile more when we're outside 8

Respecting the countryside 11

Using this guide 12

Walk 1 Crook o' Lune and Caton **14**

Walk 2 Lancaster: City, River
and Canal **20**

Photos Scenes from the walks 26

Walk 3 Gisburn Forest **28**

Walk 4 Abbeystead and Wyresdale **34**

Photos Wildlife interest 40

Walk 5 Dunsop Bridge and Dunsop
Valley **42**

Walk 6 Grizedale **48**

Walk 7 Salterforth
and Barnoldswick **54**

Photos Cafés and pubs 60

Walk 8 Garstang and Greenhalgh
Castle **62**

Walk 9 Beacon Fell **68**

Walk 10 Edisford Bridge and the
River Ribble **74**

Credits 80

Map symbols Front cover flap

Accessibility and
what to take Back cover flap

Walk locations Inside front cover

Your next adventure? Inside back cover

Walk 1

CROOK
O' LUNE AND
CATON

Distance
4 miles / 6.4km

Time
2½ hours CATCH A BUS

Start/Finish
Denny Beck car park

Parking LA2 9HQ
Denny Beck car park,
south of Halton Bridge

Cafés/pubs
Crook o' Lune, Caton
and Halton

Lovely old railway
path to Crook o'
Lune beauty spot

Page 14

Walk 2

Distance
4.5 miles / 7.25 km

Time
3 hours *GO BY TRAIN*

Start/Finish
Lune Aqueduct
car park

Parking LA1 3UA
Lune Aqueduct
car park, Caton Road,
Lancaster

Cafés/pubs
Lancaster

Canalside walk to historic Lancaster and riverside return

Works

Page 20

Walk 3

Distance
2.25 miles / 3.6 km

Time
1½ hours

Start/Finish
Stocks Reservoir car
park

Parking BB7 4TS
Stocks Reservoir,
School Ln/ Hole House
Ln junction

Cafés/pubs
Nearest at Gisburn
Forest Hub

Beautiful reservoir picnic site and lovely woodland walking

St James' Church
(foundations)

Hole Ho

Page 28

Walk 4

Distance
2.9 miles / 4.6km

Time
2 hours

Start/Finish
Abbeystead

Parking LA2 9BH
Stoops Bridge car park,
Abbeystead

Cafés/pubs
Awcock's kiosk (self-
service) near ➊

Scenic Wyresdale wander; amazing views from hilltop church

Abbeystead
Stoops Bridge
Home Farm
Hinbe
Woo

Page 34

Walk 5

DUNSOP BRIDGE AND DUNSOP VALLEY

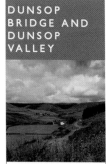

Distance
5 miles/8.1km

Time
3 hours

Start/Finish
Dunsop Bridge

Parking BB7 3BB
Dunsop Bridge
car park

Cafés/pubs
Puddleducks Tea
Rooms, Dunsop Bridge

Fine valley walk
into the heart
of Bowland's
stunning
moorland

Page 42

Walk 6

GRIZEDALE

Distance
5.3 miles/8.5km

Time
3½ hours

Start/Finish
Grizedale Head
car park

Parking PR3 1UJ
Grizedale Head
car park

Cafés/pubs
Nearest at Wyresdale
Park and Scorton

Country lane
circuit of Nicky
Nook and
wooded valley
walk

Page 48

Walk 7

SALTERFORTH AND BARNOLDSWICK

Distance
3.75 miles/6km

Time
2½ hours *CATCH A BUS*

Start/Finish
Salterforth

Parking BB18 5TT
Canalside car park

Cafés/pubs
Anchor Inn,
Salterforth;
Barnoldswick

Great views from
park high point
bookended by
colourful canal
stroll

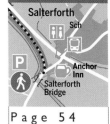

Page 54

Walk 8

GARSTANG AND GREENHALGH CASTLE

Distance
3.1 miles/5km

Time
2 hours CATCH A BUS

Start/Finish
Garstang

Parking PR3 1EB
High Street car park

Cafés/pubs
Garstang

Lush riverside and canalside walking from the gateway to Bowland

Page 62

Walk 9

BEACON FELL

Distance
2.5 miles/4km

Time
1½ hours

Start/Finish
Beacon Fell Country Park

Parking PR3 2NJ
Carwags car park

Cafés/pubs
Beacon Fell Visitor Centre café

Woodland sculpture trail and epic views from fell summit

Page 68

Walk 10

EDISFORD BRIDGE AND THE RIVER RIBBLE

Distance
5.3 miles/8.5km

Time
3½ hours GO BY TRAIN CATCH A BUS

Start/Finish
Edisford Bridge, Clitheroe

Parking BB7 2FE
Edisford Road car park

Cafés/pubs
Edisford Bridge; Great Mitton

A riparian ramble along the Ribble with a halfway pub stop

Page 74

GETTING OUTSIDE
IN THE FOREST OF BOWLAND

> **"**The hen harrier is the symbol of the AONB, and if you are really lucky you might be able to spot one**"**

OS Champion
Rory Southworth

River Dunsop near Dunsop Bridge

A very warm welcome to the new Short Walks Made Easy guide to the Forest of Bowland – what a fantastic selection of leisurely walks we have for you!

Located in north Lancashire and established in 1964, the Forest of Bowland Area of Outstanding Natural Beauty covers 310 square miles of upland countryside between Lancaster and Clitheroe, bounded by the M6 (west), the Ribble Valley (south and east) and the River Lune (north).

Today, the word 'forest' is associated with expanses of trees, and we have included wonderful woodland walks at Beacon Fell, Gisburn Forest and Grizedale, but the 'Forest' prefix in regard to Bowland derives from the medieval term for a royal hunting ground. By the 14th century, the land was used exclusively by the Lords of Bowland and their aristocratic friends to hunt wild boar, deer and wolves. You can imagine the scene looking out from the fell-top viewpoint on the Dunsop Bridge walk into the heart of Bowland's stunning heather moorland.

The hen harrier is the symbol of the AONB, and if you are really lucky you might be able to spot one of these rare raptors. But you are almost guaranteed to see mute swans gliding along the canal at Salterforth, to take delight in the hedgerow dog roses on the outing from Edisford Bridge, and be fascinated by the grizzly history of Lancaster Castle.

Rory Southworth, OS Champion

WE SMILE MORE WHEN WE'RE OUTSIDE

Bluebells at Abbeystead

Whether it's a short walk during our lunch break or a full day's outdoor adventure, we know that a good dose of fresh air is just the tonic we all need.

At Ordnance Survey (OS), we're passionate about helping more people to get outside more often. It sits at the heart of everything we do, and through our products and services, we aim to help you lead an active outdoor lifestyle, so that you can live longer, stay younger and enjoy life more.

We firmly believe the outdoors is for everyone, and we want to help you find the very best Great Britain has to offer. We are blessed with an island that is beautiful and unique, with a rich and varied landscape. There are coastal paths to meander along, woodlands to explore, countryside to roam, and cities to uncover. Our trusted source of inspirational content is bursting with ideas for places to go, things to do and easy beginner's guides on how to get started.

It can be daunting when you're new to something, so we want to bring you the know-how from the people who live and breathe the outdoors. To help guide us, our team of awe-inspiring OS Champions share their favourite places to visit, hints and tips for outdoor adventures, as well as tried and tested accessible, family- and wheelchair-friendly routes. We hope that you will feel inspired to spend more time outside and reap the physical and mental health benefits that the outdoors has to offer. With our handy guides, paper and digital mapping, and exciting new apps, we can be with you every step of the way.

To find out more visit os.uk/getoutside

RESPECTING
THE COUNTRYSIDE

You can't beat getting outside in the British countryside, but it's vital that we leave no trace when we're enjoying the great outdoors.

Let's make sure that generations to come can enjoy the countryside just as we do.

 Leave no trace

 Keep dogs under control; bin and bag waste

 Do not light fires; only BBQ at official sites

 Leave gates as you find them

 Keep to footpaths and open access land

 Plan ahead for your trip

For more details please visit
www.gov.uk/countryside-code

USING THIS GUIDE

Easy-to-follow Forest of Bowland walks for all

Before setting off

Check the walk information panel to plan your outing

- Consider using **Public transport** where flagged. If driving, note the satnav postcode for the car park under **Parking**

- The suggested **Time** is based on a gentle pace

- Note the availability of **Cafés**, tearooms and pubs, and **Toilets**

Terrain and hilliness

- **Terrain** indicates the nature of the route surface

- Any rises and falls are noted under **Hilliness**

Walking with your dog?

- This panel states where **Dogs** must be on a lead and how many stiles there are – in case you need to lift your dog

- Keep dogs on leads where there are livestock and between April and August in forest and on moorland where there are ground-nesting birds

A perfectly pocket-sized walking guide

- Handily sized for ease of use on each walk

- When not being read, it fits nicely into a pocket...

- ...so between points, put this book in the pocket of your coat, trousers or day sack and enjoy your stroll in glorious national park countryside – we've made it pocket-sized for a reason!

Flexibility of route presentation to suit all readers

- **Not comfortable map reading?** Then use the simple-to-follow route profile and accompanying route description and pictures

- **Happy to map read?** New-look walk mapping makes it easier for you to focus on the route and the points of interest along the way

- **Read the insightful Did you know?, Local legend, Stories behind the walk** and **Nature notes** to help you make the most of your day out and to enjoy all that each walk has to offer

OS information about the walk

- Many of the features and symbols shown are taken from Ordnance Survey's celebrated **Explorer** mapping, designed to help people across Great Britain enjoy leisure time spent outside

- National Grid reference for the start point
- Explorer sheet map covering the route

The easy-to-use walk map

- **Large-scale** mapping for ultra-clear route finding

- **Numbered points** at key turns along the route that tie in with the route instructions and respective points marked on the profile

- **Pictorial symbols** for intuitive map reading, see Map Symbols on the front cover flap

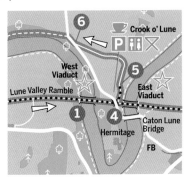

The simple-to-follow walk profile

- Progress easily along the route using the illustrative profile, it has **numbered points** for key turning points and **graduated distance** markers

- Easy-read **route directions** with turn-by-turn detail

- Reassuring **route photographs** for each numbered point

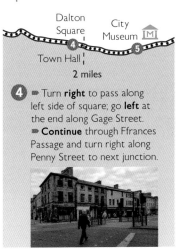

WALK 1

CATCH A BUS

THE CROOK O'LUNE AND CATON

The Crook o' Lune was immortalised by celebrated artist JMW Turner (1775-1851) in his painting depicting the horseshoe bend in the river beneath the pastured hills, with Hornby Castle and Ingleborough in the distance. It's a view that has inspired so many, including poets William Wordsworth and Thomas Gray. A young William Wilberforce declared the view to be "the finest of a kind I ever beheld".

The demise of the railway has enabled the Lune Valley Ramble from Lancaster to Caton and this route utilises the tree-lined track from Halton to Caton.

OS information

🚶 SD 503645
Explorer OL41

Distance
2 miles/3.2km (to Caton with bus return)
4 miles/6.4km (full route, or there and back along railway path)

Time
1¼ hours to Caton; 2½ hours (full route)

Start/Finish
Denny Beck car park

Parking LA2 9HQ
Denny Beck car park, Halton (at former Halton Station, just south of Halton Bridge)

Public toilets
Crook o' Lune car park, near ④

Cafés/pubs
Cafés at Crook o' Lune car park and Caton; pubs at Halton and Caton

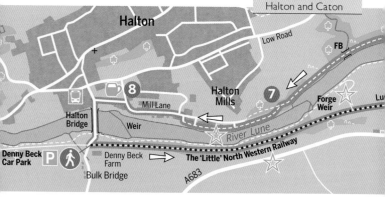

Terrain
Tarred disused railway path, pavement and lanes; woodland/riverside path beyond

Hilliness
Railway path flat; then gently undulating

Footwear
Winter 🥾
Spring/Summer/Autumn 👟

🚌 Public transport
Two-hourly bus service 81/82 from Caton back to Halton: cumbria.gov.uk/buses/81/

♿ Accessibility
Wheelchair and pushchair friendly on railway path and pavement

🐕 Dogs
 Welcome but keep on leads on shared-use cycle path along old railway. No stiles

Did you know? The woodland around the Hermitage Field, near the visitor centre, has been opened up as a 'Life for a Life' area, where trees are planted in memory of loved ones. The trees, which include hawthorn, hazel, silver birch and wild cherry, help with climate change and wildlife conservation and give mourners a peaceful place to remember their loved ones.

Local legend Queen's Well, just south of the Crook o' Lune, has several legendary associations. It is said that Mary Queen of Scots rested here on her way to Bolton Castle, where she was imprisoned. The story inspired the poem *Queen Marie's Well* by 19th-century author and arts critic, Henry Chorley. Stories also associate Eleanor of Castile, the wife of King Edward I, with the place.

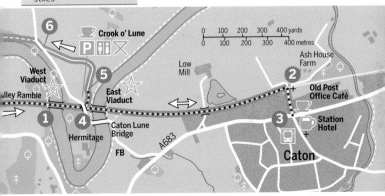

STORIES BEHIND THE WALK

☆ **The Lune-Wyre Transfer Scheme** This scheme, operating between Forge Weir and Abbeystead, involves transferring up to 62 million gallons of water to meet any exceptional need throughout the county. In 1984 a build-up of methane gas caused an explosion killing sixteen visitors (see the Abbeystead Disaster, Walk 4).

☆ **Forge Weir** The walk passes Forge Weir ⑦ on the return to Halton. Here, the Environment Agency operates a fish counter to monitor the numbers of salmon and sea trout, which come to spawn upriver. The numbers had been dwindling in the 20th century due to disease but are now recovering.

1 mile

1 ½ mile

🅿 Denny Beck car park

➥ Keeping the old station platform on left, walk out of car park and along tarred old trackbed for 1 mile to viaduct.

① ➥ Cross West Viaduct over the Lune.
➥ Keep **straight ahead** under stone road bridge and across the East Viaduct.
➥ Continue on old railway path for almost 1 mile to a chapel.

☆ The Caton-Lune Road Bridge

The Grade II-listed three-arched road bridge constructed using sandstone ashlar was built in 1883 to replace an earlier one which had become structurally unsound. This earlier one was a privately owned toll bridge, known as the Penny Bridge.

☆ The 'Little' North Western Railway

The walk starts at the old Halton Station along the former trackbed of the 'Little' North Western Railway, which connected Skipton and Morecambe via Halton and Lancaster. The two great viaducts that carry the railway over the Crook o' Lune were built to designs by Edmund Sharpe in 1849. The six-arched West Viaduct and the five-arched East Viaduct were once single track but were modified in 1882 to accommodate dual-running. The Grade II-listed structures were both refurbished in the early 21st century. Like most disused railways the line was closed by the Beeching cuts of the 1960s.

☆ The 'Little' North Western Railway

Crook o' Lune ☆ ☆

West Viaduct ☐🅿️☕ 🚻 East Viaduct ⊢ 1½ miles ⊣ **+** ⊢ 2 miles ⊣

☕ Station Hotel ☕ Old Post Office Café

2 ➡ On reaching chapel, turn **right** along lane signed Local Facilities and Brookhouse to Caton village centre. The lane comes to the Station Hotel and the Old Post Office Café.

3 ➡ Retrace steps back to old railway path and go **left** along it.
➡ Cross the East Viaduct.

4 ➡ On far side of viaduct turn **right** along the middle of three paths.
➡ Pass to the **right** of Crook o' Lune car park (unless using the café or toilets) to reach picnic site.

Walk 1 Crook o' Lune and Caton **17**

NATURE NOTES

The old railway track is lined by lush verges and trees and bushes of all shapes and sizes. These include oak, sycamore, beech and rowan, shading thickets of the pretty dog rose with red campion, herb-robert and primroses below. Watch out for the many spiral, wheel-shaped spiders' webs clinging to the metalwork of the viaducts. They belong to the orb-weaver spiders, common but very colourful little creatures.

Bats are common in the area. If it's nearing sunset you may spy what seems at first glance to be an agitated bird darting here, there and everywhere. It's likely that it's a pipistrelle bat, a golden-brown mammal that captures and eats insects in flight. This, our smallest most agile bat, is the most common in the UK and hibernates in winter. It usually lives in tree hollows or roof spaces. Noctule and Daubenton's bats also thrive around this area.

Herb-robert

Crook o' Lune ✕

2½ miles · River Lune 🅿 🚻 ☕

River Lune 3 mil

5 ➡ Wheelchairs and pushchairs should return to Denny Beck car park along old railway path.
➡ Go through gate at far side of picnic benches to follow a surfaced path across meadows to reach another gate.

6 ➡ Through gate, turn **right** along country lane. Turn **left** in 50 yards to go through kissing-gate.
➡ Descend to river along narrow path that continues, mostly by riverbank, to reach steps.

Pipistrelle bat

Orb-weaver spider

Red campion

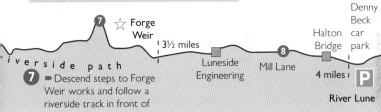

☆ Forge Weir

Denny Beck car park

Halton Bridge

3½ miles

r i v e r s i d e   p a t h

Luneside Engineering

Mill Lane

4 miles

7 ➥ Descend steps to Forge Weir works and follow a riverside track in front of flats.
➥ Turn **right** by Luneside Engineering, then **left** along Mill Lane.
➥ Ignore Mill Lane Mews but bend right with Mill Lane to next junction.

P River Lune

8 ➥ Turn **left** at T-junction.
➥ At next junction, turn **left** again and cross Denny Beck Bridge to car park.

WALK 2

GO BY TRAIN

LANCASTER: CITY, RIVER AND CANAL

Lancaster is one of the North's great places, rich in history, both of royalty and harsh justice. On this walk you can admire the impressive Lune Aqueduct and follow the tree-lined canal, high above the city, all the way to the centre, where the castle awaits you with its dungeons and haunted courtrooms. You then come to the quayside where great ships used to dock bringing cargo from all over the world – a maritime museum here is well worth visiting before the return journey along the banks of the River Lune.

OS information

🚶 SD 487637
Explorer 296

Distance
4.5 miles/7.25km

Time
3 hours

Start/Finish
Lune Aqueduct car park

Parking LA1 3UA
Lune Aqueduct car park, Caton Road, Lancaster

Public toilets
Across the road at ❸, in the Nelson Street car park

Cafés/pubs
Lancaster

Terrain
Canal towpath, city pavement and tarred riverside path

Hilliness
One gradual ramp up to canal; otherwise flat

Did you know? A packet boat passenger service used to operate on the Lancaster Canal between Preston and Kendal and, although it took 10 hours, many passengers still used it several years after the coming of the railways.

Local legend With such a grizzly past it's no wonder that ghosts are said to roam various parts of Lancaster Castle. One of many Catholic priests hanged here for treason is said to wander around with a noose around his neck. Old Demdike (Elizabeth Southerns), one of the Pendle Witches, also haunts the place. Some visitors have heard whispering voices and the jangling of keys; others have been barged in the back and turned around to find no-one was there.

Footwear
Year round

Public transport
Lancaster is on the West Coast Main Line railway. Bus service 81 goes from Lancaster bus station to the Aqueduct car park: cumbria.gov.uk/buses/81/

Accessibility
Wheelchairs and pushchairs throughout

Dogs Welcome but keep on leads. No stiles

STORIES BEHIND THE WALK

Lancaster Castle The current Norman castle is believed to be 11th century. Owned by the Duchy of Lancaster, a title which has since the late 14th century meant the monarch, the castle has long been associated with dark deeds. It was used as a prison and courts of 'justice' from 1196. Over two hundred citizens have been executed, including the so-called Pendle Witches, also many Catholic priests who were charged by Elizabeth I with High Treason. Many thousands of the townsfolk would gather outside the castle walls to watch the executions. The castle ceased to be a prison in 2011 and today is open to visitors. Frequent tours allow you to go back through its dark history.

☆ **The Lune Aqueduct**
One of the first things you'll see on this walk is the majestic five-arched Lune Aqueduct, which carries the Lancaster Canal over the River Lune, some 60 feet below. It was designed by John Rennie and completed in 1797. Problems with the foundations of the Lune Aqueduct swallowed up much of the money allocated to other sections of the canal.

Lune Aqueduct ☆   1 mile

ramp   ½ mile   ☆ **L a n c a s t e r C a n a l**

P Lune Aqueduct car park

➡ The route starts from a gateway at the back of the car park.

1 ➡ Follow a good path through a grassy little nature reserve with shrubs and ponds.
➡ Turn **left** under aqueduct and then **left** again on tarred path to the foot of steps.

2 ➡ Ignore steps but go **right** then immediately **left** up tarred ramp to reach canal towpath.
➡ Turn **right**, away from aqueduct, along tree-lined towpath.
➡ Enjoy 1¾-mile stroll to reach bridge opposite Lancaster Cathedral.

☆ The Romans

The commanding position on a hill above the River Lune was appreciated by the Romans, who established a fort here in CE 43 to repel the warring Picts and Scots. A small town would have been established around the fort. The Romans abandoned Lancaster in the fifth century but you can still see the ruins of their bathhouse near the castle.

☆ The Lancaster Canal

The canal was orignally planned to run between Kendal and Westhoughton and carry limestone from Cumbria and coal from the Lancashire mines. An aqueduct over the Ribble near Preston had to be shelved for financial reasons and the north and south sections were only linked by a tramway. The southern section was eventually curtailed and joined the Leeds–Liverpool Canal at Johnson's Hillock near Chorley. By the middle of the 20th century the canal had become neglected and some sections were filled in, others were rendered impassable by the construction of motorways.

Lancaster Cathedral ✝

3

☆ **Lancaster Canal**
1½ miles

🅿 🚻
Nelson Street car park

Dalton Square

City Museum 🏛

4 Town Hall **5**
2 miles

3 ➤ Pass **under** the Joseph Clayton Bridge and immediately turn **right** into Canal Quarter (Nelson Street) car park.
➤ Pass along right-hand side to exit onto Nelson Street.
➤ Turn **left** and walk to Dalton Square by town hall.

4 ➤ Turn **right** to pass along left side of square; go **left** at the end along Gage Street.
➤ **Continue** through Ffrances Passage and turn right along Penny Street to next junction.

NATURE NOTES

Cormorant, little egret, grey heron and green sandpiper can be seen by the River Lune at Lancaster. Cormorants are quite large, black-feathered birds and in open water are capable of diving 150 feet. Their agility and their hooked beaks make them very proficient at catching fish.

The yellow blooms and spear-shaped leaves of yellow flag iris can be seen on the banks of the canal and in some of the ponds in the little nature reserve beneath the aqueduct. The leaves of the iris provide a sheltered habitat for many birds, including swans, coots and mallards.

Red campion can be found on the verges of the Lune-side footpath, often mingling with buttercups. The tall plants have downy stems and pretty five-petalled pink flowers which bloom in late spring or early summer. The flowers are important for pollinating insects like small tortoiseshell, red admiral and meadow brown butterflies, as well as bees and hoverflies.

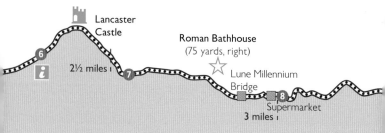

Lancaster Castle

6

i 2½ miles

7

Roman Bathhouse (75 yards, right)

☆

Lune Millennium Bridge

8

Supermarket

3 miles

5 ➥ Go **left** along Market Street, passing to **left** of the impressive City Museum building.
➥ Cross **straight over** China Street (A6) to next junction.

6 ➥ Turn **right** up Castle Hill and follow it to junction just past Lancaster Castle's keep.
➥ Here, take Long Marsh Lane, signed to the railway station, stopping at railway bridge.

Cormorant

Yellow flag iris

Red admiral butterfly

Red campion and buttercup

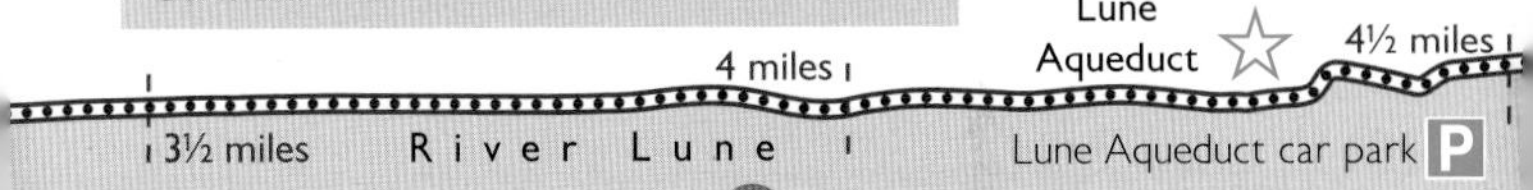

7 ➡ Turn **right** just before bridge onto a tarred path that circles **right** through parkland trees to reach the river by Lune Millennium Bridge.

➡ Turn **right** along the riverside to reach a large supermarket.

8 ➡ Beyond this (car park, right) follow path **right** then **left** to use underpass beneath A589.

➡ **Keep forward** onto tarred riverside path, signed Caton and the Lune Aqueduct, for 1½ miles to return to aqueduct.

➡ Retrace steps beneath it; turn **right** through nature reserve to car park.

This page (clockwise): Leeds and Liverpool canal at Salterforth; sunset in Forest of Bowland; Lancaster City Museum; Letcliffe Park sculpture trail
Opposite (clockwise): Brennand Valley; Gisburn Forest; decorated marker near Christ Church, Abbeystead

26

GISBURN FOREST

Gisburn Forest lies in the north-east corner of the Forest of Bowland, tucked between the wild Bowland heather moors and the chequered fields of the Hodder Valley. A good path network allows visitors the freedom to roam through the woods. Although most of the trees are either spruce or pine, you will not notice as the tracks are often lined with broad-leaved trees, which soften the scenery and let in the light for wildflowers and shrubs. For bird lovers there's much to see on the shores of Stocks Reservoir.

OS information

 SD 732565
Explorer OL41

Distance
2.25 miles / 3.6 km

Time
1½ hours

Start/Finish
Stocks Reservoir car park

Parking BB7 4TS
Stocks Reservoir car park, at junction of School Lane and Hole House Lane

Public toilets
Nearest at Gisburn Forest Hub, about 1¾ miles east from walk start along Hole House Lane

Cafés/pubs
Café at Gisburn Forest Hub

Terrain
Good, firm, stony forest tracks

Hilliness	
Gently undulating	

Hilliness
Gently undulating

Footwear
Year round

 Public transport
None

 Accessibility

Accessible for all to
4, after which follow
alternative route
for wheelchairs and
pushchairs

Dogs
Welcome but
keep on leads due
to shared-use forest
tracks with cyclists.
No stiles

Did you know? The Gisburn Forest area was once part of the manor of the House of Percy, one of the most powerful noble families in the North of England following the Norman Invasion.

Local legend The Ribblesdale Arms, a former coaching inn at nearby Gisburn, closed its doors at the turn of the 21st century, ending nearly 400 years of life as an inn. But the building is said to be haunted by its dark past. The name of the ghost is Mary. One night Mary is alleged to have been assaulted by Lord Ribblesdale, who then pushed her down the stairs. Mary hanged herself and it is said that her spirit regularly haunted Room 13.

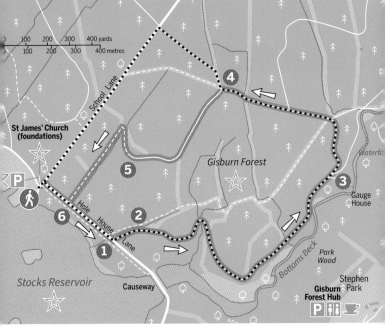

STORIES BEHIND THE WALK

☆ **Stocks-in-Bowland** Unfortunately the village of Stocks-in-Bowland, which also served the Dalehead Valley, was submerged beneath the waters of Stocks Reservoir. It consisted of a handful of farms, a post office, a smithy, a church and the New Inn. Although it stood above the proposed water level, St James' Church, along with farms in the upper valley, had to be demolished. You can see the foundations by the car park at the start of the walk. Much of the masonry and many of the fittings were used in the new church, built nearby on higher ground to the east. Date stones moved from the demolished cottages and farms can be seen by the old church.

☆ **Stocks Reservoir**
Stocks Reservoir was created by the Fylde Water Board in 1932 by flooding the Dalehead Valley. A railway, built from the site of the dam to the nearby hamlet of Tosside, carried quarried material for the dam and a temporary village housed up to 500 men at the height of the construction. The reservoir was opened by HRH Prince George in July 1932.

Stocks Reservoir car park

☆ Stocks Reservoir

☆ **G i s b u r n   F o r e s t**

1 ½ m

➡ Leave car park and turn **right** along road for ¼ mile to T-junction with forest track. (NB the footpath running parallel to it has no useable exit at ❶ for pushchair and wheelchair users.)

☆ **St James' Church** (foundations)

❶ ➡ Turn **left** along track for 125 yards to a fork.

☆ **Gisburn Forest** Covering an area of 2,955 acres, Gisburn Forest is the largest wooded area in Lancashire. The land, which was in the Stocks Reservoir catchment area, was leased to the then Forestry Commission (now Forestry England) by the Fylde Water Board (now United Utilities) in 1949. Most of the forest is planted with Sitka spruce and Scots pine but there is an area of ancient woodland known as Park Wood, south-east of Bottoms Beck. The 20-acre broad-leaved wood is classified as a Biological Heritage Site. Two prehistoric barrows are sited on the banks of Dob Dale Beck in the northern regions of the forest.

☆ **Sport and leisure in Gisburn Forest**

Although it is a working forest, Forestry England has spent much money on promoting it as a leisure facility. There is a visitor hub at the 16th-century former farmhouse of Stephen Park. Here there is a good café and a bike hire centre to supplement a large network of footpaths and mountain-bike trails.

☆ **G i s b u r n   F o r e s t**

1 mile

2 ➡ Stay **right**, ignoring left fork.
➡ **Continue** along main forest track, winding though trees for ¾ mile to meet two closely spaced right forks.

3 ➡ Ignore both forks and **keep forward** as the track bends left at a crossways.
➡ **Continue** for another ⅓ mile, ignoring any side turns, to a broad track junction.

NATURE NOTES

There are many birds on the reservoir and hides have been built to watch them. In the spring the oystercatcher, curlew, lapwing, redshank and snipe arrive. In summer you should see hundreds of black-headed gulls, which breed on the islands. These noisy, quarrelsome birds eat anything they can get their beaks on. In the winter the reservoir is visited by goldeneye, pochard, wigeon and pintail ducks. Osprey are fairly regular visitors to the area. Fully grown, these large hawks have a wingspan of around 6 feet. They fly across the water to spy their prey. Once found they hover above before diving feet first to spear the fish with their long curved talons.

The forest is largely planted with Sitka spruce, the largest of all spruce trees. It was first imported to the British Isles from the west coast of North America – its name derives from the region of Sitka in Alaska. This spruce grows quickly in poor soils, where it can reach over 300 feet in height.

Above: Sitka spruce
Opposite page
Top: pintail
Middle: black-headed gull
Bottom: lapwing

4
¦ 1½ miles

☆ Gisburn Forest

4 ➡ Walkers without pushchairs or wheelchairs fork **left** and follow track for ⅓ mile to its end.
➡ Pushchair and wheelchair users branch **right** with main track. Follow it to road and there turn **left** back to the car park.

5 ➡ At track terminus go **straight ahead** into trees on a narrow path that widens as it winds down to road.

Above: osprey
Below: curlew

Stocks
Reservoir ☆

☆ **G i s b u r n   F o r e s t**   ⁵   ⌐ 2 miles   ⁶

Stocks Reservoir car park [P]
[⊠]

St James' Church ☆
(foundations)

6 ⬛ Turn **right** along the lane
or through the gateway
to use the aforementioned
parallel path back to the car
park.

Bird hide, Stocks Reservoir

ABBEYSTEAD AND WYRESDALE

This walk is almost entirely across the Abbeystead Estate, owned by the Duke of Westminster (the Grosvenor family). You'll see the fine 19th-century stone buildings of the village, stroll with delight by the banks of the River Wyre, and pass an old church on a hill. The church has a wonderful view of the Wyre Valley and the wild heather ridge of Hawthornthwaite Fell, which stretches across the horizon. Should you have a mind to, you can end the walk with a Wallings ice cream made in Bowland.

OS information

🚶 SD 563543
Explorer OL41

Distance
2.9 miles / 4.6 km

Time
2 hours

Start/Finish
Abbeystead

Parking LA2 9BH
Stoops Bridge car park, Doeholme Rake, Abbeystead

Public toilets
None

Cafés/pubs
Awcock's refreshment kiosk (self-service), roadside near ➊

Terrain
Village lane, field paths and tracks

Hilliness
One climb **5** to **6**, otherwise gently undulating

Footwear
Winter
Spring/Summer/ Autumn

Public transport
None

Accessibility
Not accessible to wheelchairs; all-terrain pushchairs in dry conditions to **5**

Dogs
Welcome but keep on leads due to livestock. Nine stiles

Did you know? The Duchy of Westminster was created by Queen Victoria in 1874 for Hugh Grosvenor, the 3rd Marquess of Westminster. It is the most recent dukedom bestowed on anyone not related to the royal family. Hugh Grosvenor, the current and 7th Duke, is godfather to Prince George of Wales.

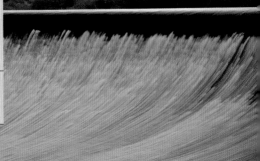

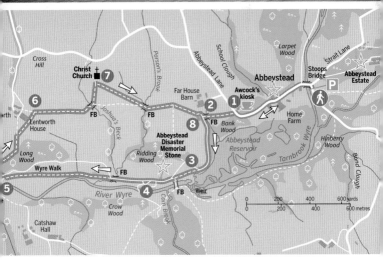

STORIES BEHIND THE WALK

☆ **Abbeystead village** The name Abbeystead is derived from 'the site of the abbey'. There was a short-lived presence of Cistercian monks from Furness Abbey between 1192 and 1204. It is believed that the monks' house was near the confluence of the Marshaw and Tarnbrook Wyre, although another theory has it near the current Cawthorne's Endowed School. The original schoolhouse dated from 1674 but was rebuilt in 1877.

☆ **Abbeystead Estate** The great Elizabethan-styled mansion of Abbeystead House, which you can see from Stoops Bridge, was built as a shooting lodge for the 4th Earl of Sefton. The hills of Bowland are known for grouse shooting and the Abbeystead Estate holds the record for the most red grouse shot in one day — nearly 3,000 birds were shot by just eight gunmen. In 1855 Lancaster Corporation built the current reservoir to supply water to the many mills downriver.

Abbeystead village ☆

Far House (farm)

½ mile

(walker) Tarnbrook Wyre

(P) Stoops Bridge car park

(1) Awcock's kiosk

(2) ➧ Through gate and over wooden footbridge, turn **left** along concrete track by barn.
➧ It runs by Bank Wood. Take **left** fork stony track and go through estate gate to continue past dam and outflow of Abbeystead Reservoir.

(3) Weir

➧ Turn **left** out of car park then **left** again along road through village. Walk to right-hand bend in lane (Awcock's refreshments round corner).

(1) ➧ Turn **left** over stile or through gate.
➧ Head **across** field towards barns to left of the main buildings of Far House farm.

☆ **The Abbeystead Disaster** On 23 May 1984, 44 people, mostly from the Lancashire village of St Michael's on Wyre, were being shown around the valve house in Abbeystead. It had been built as part of the Lune/Wyre Transfer Scheme and Geoff Seed, a senior North West Water Authority official, wanted to allay fears about flooding on the Wyre. Suddenly an explosion occurred in the building resulting from a build-up of methane in an empty pipe. It was released by the sudden pressure of water from the pumps as they were switched on and instantly ignited. Sixteen people were killed, including Geoff Seed.

✝ **Christ Church**

Standing aloof on a pastured hillside overlooking the River Wyre, Christ Church was first built in 1733. It was restored and modified in 1894 by John Douglas, who added a chancel, vestry and south porch. A carved pulpit is dated 1684. The church is often known as the Shepherds' Church – some of the stained-glass windows depict sheep and shepherds and an inscription on the gate says, 'I am the door of the sheep'.

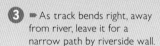

Abbeystead Disaster
☆ Memorial Stone

4

...eystead ...ervoir

1 mile

River Wyre

5

Long Bridge

3 ➡ As track bends right, away from river, leave it for a narrow path by riverside wall.
➡ The path leads back to main concrete track, later passing Abbeystead Disaster Memorial Stone.
➡ **Continue** to track junction.

4 ➡ Where concrete track veers down to river, keep **straight ahead** on wide stony track.
➡ In ¼ mile, leave track as it veers right to continue **ahead** on waymarked path.
➡ After climbing a low bank towards woods, come to Long Bridge.

NATURE NOTES

Curlew and lapwing are frequently seen in the pastures on the walk below Wyresdale church **7**. Lapwings are a crested black and white bird with broad, rounded wings. They are in decline in Britain and have been put on the red list of endangered species.

The woods around the river are generally broad-leaved, with oak, horse chestnut, silver birch, rowan sycamore and ash. We all recognise the sycamore as synonymous with Britain but it's not a native and was imported in the early 16th century from southern Europe where it thrives high in the mountains. It's an acer, relative to the maple, which also has the same five-fingered leaves. The tree has been successful here in that it grows up to 100 feet high and spreads rapidly through its winged fruits.

Roe deer thrive in the local woodland. They are very shy and if they spot you first you won't see them. This small deer, up to 2 foot 6 inches at shoulder height, has a reddish-brown colour with a white rump in summer, turning to a greyish or dark brown hue in winter. The male has short antlers.

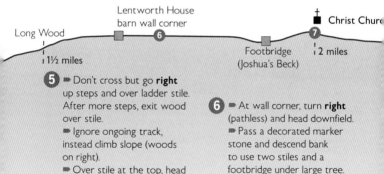

Long Wood

Lentworth House
barn wall corner
6

† Christ Churc
■ Christ Churc **7**

Footbridge
(Joshua's Beck)

| 1½ miles

| 2 miles

5 ➠ Don't cross but go **right** up steps and over ladder stile. After more steps, exit wood over stile.
➠ Ignore ongoing track, instead climb slope (woods on right).
➠ Over stile at the top, head for right-hand side of barn ahead and reach wall corner beyond.

6 ➠ At wall corner, turn **right** (pathless) and head downfield.
➠ Pass a decorated marker stone and descend bank to use two stiles and a footbridge under large tree.
➠ Beyond these head **half left** towards church on the hill.

Roe deer

Above: horse chestnut leaves
Below: sycamore leaves

Abbeystead
village ☆

Footbridge   Far House (farm) | 2½ miles
(arson's Brook)   Tarnbrook Wyre   P

Stoops Bridge car park

7 ➤ From church veer **right**, away from wall and continue over field to cross stile and footbridge at far end.
➤ In next field, aim for farm buildings ahead. Over stile, go **half right** towards barns to right of farm complex.

8 ➤ Go over stile in front of barn, turn **right** for a few paces then go **left** over the wooden footbridge ②.
➤ Retrace steps across the field and turn **right** along the lane through the village.

Opposite (clockwise): common pipistrelle; sycamore samaras. This page (clockwise): brown hare; dog rose; hen harrier; osprey; ling and small copper

WALK 5

DUNSOP BRIDGE AND DUNSOP VALLEY

This walk takes you into the heart of Bowland, up into a wild and beautiful valley with high moors above you and a crystal stream rushing over boulders on its long journey to the Irish Sea. United Utilities provide notice boards to help you understand the various structures – intakes, weirs and the odd stone building. You'll probably see and hear the cackling red grouse, maybe a raptor such as a merlin or hen harrier and, if it's late summer, the scene will be covered with the purple-pink hues of the heather.

OS information

🧭 SD 661501
Explorer OL41

Distance
5 miles/8.1km

Time
3 hours

Start/Finish Dunsop Bridge

Parking BB7 3BB Dunsop Bridge car park

Public toilets
In car park

Cafés/pubs
Puddleducks Tea Rooms, Dunsop Bridge

Terrain
Tarred lane; short section of gravelled path

Hilliness
Outward route gently rising, the return gently descending; short climb to viewpoint

Footwear
Year round 👟

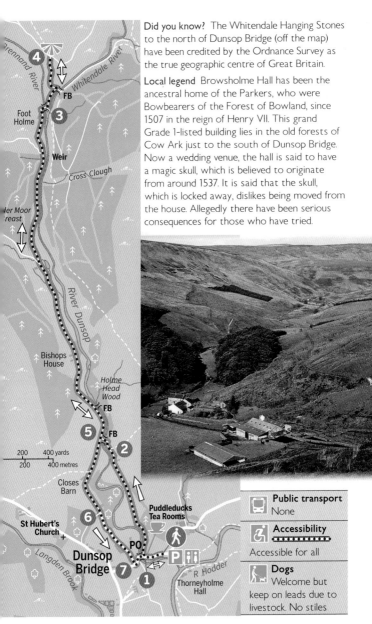

Did you know? The Whitendale Hanging Stones to the north of Dunsop Bridge (off the map) have been credited by the Ordnance Survey as the true geographic centre of Great Britain.

Local legend Browsholme Hall has been the ancestral home of the Parkers, who were Bowbearers of the Forest of Bowland, since 1507 in the reign of Henry VII. This grand Grade 1-listed building lies in the old forests of Cow Ark just to the south of Dunsop Bridge. Now a wedding venue, the hall is said to have a magic skull, which is believed to originate from around 1537. It is said that the skull, which is locked away, dislikes being moved from the house. Allegedly there have been serious consequences for those who have tried.

Public transport
None

Accessibility
Accessible for all

Dogs
Welcome but keep on leads due to livestock. No stiles

STORIES BEHIND THE WALK

☆ **Water Supply** In the 1880s Blackburn's councillors were in need of water to supply their factories and mills, and they cast their eyes towards the remote valleys north of Dunsop Bridge. They considered two reservoirs, one at Whitendale and the other at Brennand, feeder streams of the Dunsop and Hodder rivers, but the engineers told them that the ground wasn't stable enough for dam construction. Instead they built intakes and pipelines to take water directly from the rivers. You'll see the structures on the route.

☆ **Flooding of the Valleys**

On 8 August 1967 almost 4½ inches of rain fell in 90 minutes. The swollen streams of Whitendale and Brennand carried boulders down the Dunsop and Hodder valleys, destroying seven bridges, half a mile of road and severing the water pipeline. In the same storm, raging waters from the River Roeburn destroyed many houses in the village of Wray in the north of Bowland and left Mallowdale Pike with a great scar. The intake was rebuilt in 1973.

Puddleducks
☕ Tea Rooms

Footbridge

½ mile

1 mile

🚶 🅿 Dunsop Bridge car park

🚻

① ➤ From the car park, return to the road and go **right**, to Puddleducks Tea Rooms.

☆ **R i v e r D u n s o p**

① ➤ Immediately beyond Puddleducks turn **right** along tarred lane with small parking area.
➤ Follow lane to reach a stone-built house. Pass to the **left** of it.

☆ Grouse Shooting

Grouse shooting first became popular in the mid-19th century, when an expanding railway network allowed access into Britain's upland areas. One form is driven grouse shooting, where the red grouse are driven by beaters over a fixed position to create targets for the wealthy clients lying in wait. The alternative form is a walked-up shoot, where the grouse are flushed up as the shoot proceeds, usually assisted by specially trained dogs. The moorland habitat is managed for the benefits of the grouse by heather-burning to encourage new growth. The Duke of Westminster's lands in Bowland became a popular venue.

✚ The Church and the Racehorse If you visit St Hubert's Church in Dunsop Bridge you'll see a painting of a horse on the ceiling above the altar. It depicts the 1861 Derby winner Kettledrum, which was owned by Colonel Charles Towneley of nearby Thorneyholme Hall. Apparently, the church was paid for with the horse's winnings.

1½ miles   2 miles   Foot Holme   2½ miles

☆ River Dunsop

2 ➡ Fork **left** on narrower path, cross footbridge over River Dunsop and turn **right**.
➡ Walk up the valley on another tarred lane for 1½ miles (river on right) to information boards at Foot Holme.

3 ➡ At information boards **cross** river on a wide bridge.
➡ Bear **left** up the valley to next footbridge.
➡ Don't cross, but climb lane for about 300 yards to junction (viewpoint) where the outward route ends.

NATURE NOTES

The upland nature of the Dunsop, Whitendale and Brennand valleys lends itself to heathland vegetation. Ling, sometimes known as common heather, creates that purple-pink carpet we know and love on the moors of Britain. Left to its own devices it can grow up to 20 inches high, although on grouse moors it is kept short. Heather is an important source of nutrition for sheep and deer, especially when snow covers the lower-growing grasses. Unfortunately for heather, it's also a food source for the heather beetle. Its larvae feed voraciously on new growth in spring and strip the leaves resulting in bare brown patches. Occasionally there have been population explosions when huge areas of heath have been decimated.

Pride of Bowland is the hen harrier. This beautiful raptor is the current symbol of the Forest of Bowland AONB. The male bird looks very different to the female: it's mainly pale grey, including the breast and with a white underside. The female, on the other hand, is brown with a dark brown-streaked fawn underside. Hen harriers feed mostly on small mammals and birds. In Britain the hen harrier has been persecuted, almost to extinction, on grouse shooting estates where they are perceived as a threat to young grouse.

3 miles

3½ miles

☆ R i v e r   D u n s o p

4 ➡ Nearby seat makes a good place for a picnic.
➡ Return the way you came to footbridge near **2**.

5 ➡ On reaching footbridge near **2** keep **ahead** on tarred lane, which soon passes Closes Barn farm.
➡ Follow lane to next junction, with cattle grids.

Hen harrier

Heather beetle

Ling

Closes Barn

Puddleducks
Tea Rooms

5 — 4½ miles — 6 — 7

4 miles

☆ R i v e r   D u n s o p

5 miles
Dunsop Bridge car park

6 ➥ Go **straight on** to walk past a crescent of houses before coming to main village road.

7 ➥ Turn **left**, pass over village's stone bridge and back to Puddleducks, the car park beyond on left.

Walk 5 Dunsop Bridge and Dunsop Valley   47

WALK 6

GRIZEDALE

Grizedale Bridge, a 19th-century Grade II-listed structure, lies at the very edge of Bowland's heather moors, which dominate all early views on this walk. An old bridleway takes you across pasture before descending along quiet, hedge-lined lanes with flower-decked verges. Passing beneath Nicky Nook the views across Wyresdale Park are wide and spectacular reaching to Blackpool Tower and across Morecambe Bay to the Lakeland fells. The wooded walk up Grizedale makes a contrast with the reservoir in the dappled shade of the trees and rhododendrons.

OS information

☯ SD 535491
Explorer OL41

Distance
Full walk
5.3 miles/8.5km
Circuit from 🚻
3.8 miles/6km

Time
Full walk
3½ hours
Circuit from 🚻
2½ hours

Start/Finish
Grizedale Head car park. 🚻 on Snowhill Lane (see map, and read from ⑤ in text)

Parking PR3 1UJ
Grizedale Head car park. PR3 1BA Roadside parking on Snowhill Lane near junction with Higher Lane

Public toilets
At Scorton, ¾ mile along Snowhill Lane from 🚻

Cafés/pubs
Nearest is Applestore Café at Wyresdale Park, 600 yards along Snowhill Lane from 🚻; Priory Café, Scorton

Terrain
Field paths and tracks; country lanes

Hilliness
Gentle climbs and descents

Footwear
Winter 🥾
Spring/Summer/
Autumn 👟

 Public transport
None

♿ **Accessibility**
••••••••••
All-terrain wheelchair
and pushchair friendly
♿ via **6**, **7**, **8**, **4**
and **5**; path from
Grizedale Head to **4**
difficult for wheelchairs/
pushchairs

🐕 **Dogs**
Welcome but
keep on leads due to
livestock. No stiles

Did you know? The nearby Wyresdale Park Estate, owned by the Whewell family, appeared on the TV programme *Country House Rescue*, after which the estate was divided. They built a glamping site near the boating pool and some of the buildings were converted into the Applestore Café.

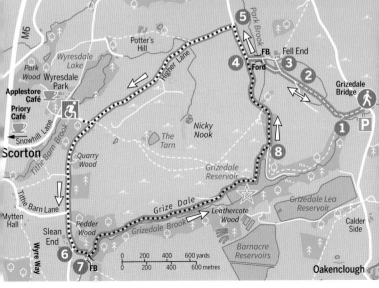

STORIES BEHIND THE WALK

☆ **The Royal Forest** People associate the word forest with trees. However, it was not always so. In medieval times a forest was a royal hunting ground. Bowland is largely comprised of heather moorland and peat bog. After the Norman Conquest the land was awarded to the de Lacy family, who later became the Lords of Bowland. By the 14th century Bowland had become a Royal Forest. The most powerful men in the land would hunt for the wild boar, wolves, wildcats and deer that roamed freely in the area. Although deer still roam, the last herd of wild deer had been wiped out by 1805.

☆ **The Reservoirs** The Grizedale Reservoir was constructed in 1866 to supply the growing coastal towns of the Fylde. Its dam is an earth embankment 70 feet high and 130 yards in length. The Grizedale Lea and Barnacre reservoirs to the south were completed by 1920 to supply the burgeoning population of the seaside resort of Blackpool. The woodland that surrounds them offers a haven for many birds.

Grizedale Head car park

½ mile

Fell End Farm

1 mile

1 ➡ From gates fork **right** on bridleway, rising over the shoulder of the hillside.
➡ Follow worn, grassy track, faint in places, though two gates.

➡ Take narrow path from the back of the car park to double gates at a path junction.

2 ➡ At second gate Fell End Farm comes into view. The bridleway aims for this.

☆ **Scorton** The roots of Scorton go back to the 17th century when it was recorded as 'Scurton', meaning farmstead near a ditch or ravine, presumably Grizedale. It once had a cotton mill powered by an underground waterwheel fed by the River Wyre. The mill closed and is now a joinery shop. There was also a railway station on the nearby West Coast Main Line but this was closed in 1939.

Snowhill Lane
Alternative start

| 1½ miles | | 2 miles | 2½ miles | Slean End |

Higher Lane

3 ➡ Near farm, watch for a gate on **left**, the start of a concessionary bridleway that avoids farmyard.
➡ This cuts a corner to farm's drive where you turn **left** to reach a lane.

4 ➡ Turn **right** along country lane for 350 yards to next junction.

NATURE NOTES

There's a possibility you might see brown hares as well as rabbits on the farmland early in the walk. The two can be distinguished by the larger hare's powerful long hind legs, long black-tipped ears and more reddish colour. The hare is thought to have been introduced from the Netherlands or Denmark, sometime in the Iron Age. Although it is mainly a nocturnal animal it can be seen in the daytime, especially around the mating season.

The meadow pipit is the most common of upland birds and loves the open habitats of the upper part of this walk, especially the heather moor above the car park. It nests on the ground in thick vegetation and feeds on insects such as spiders and craneflies.

In the hedgerows that line the country lanes you'll see the pretty pink or white dog rose among the hawthorn; also elder whose berries and flowers make lovely wine, the flowers, white and the berries, red.

Brown hare

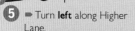

3 miles   3½ miles   ☆ Grizedale Reservoir   4 mile

7

G r i z e d a l e

5 ➧ Turn **left** along Higher Lane.
➧ It descends gradually beneath Nicky Nook (left) to pass Snowhill Lane 🄳 in 1 mile.
➧ Stay on Higher Lane for another ½ mile as it swings **left** and continues to Slean End.

6 ➧ After passing cottages, fork **left** through a gate and descend to the main bridleway in the valley bottom.

Elderberries

Top: meadow pipit
Above: white dog rose

4½ miles

Fell End Farm

5 miles

Grizedale Head car park **P**

To continue walk for wheelchairs and pushchairs, read from **4**

7 ▬ Use the gate and go **left** along a wide track through Grizedale Valley woods.
▬ After almost 1 mile it passes Grizedale Reservoir (right).
▬ 175 yards beyond end of reservoir arm, meet a track junction.

8 ▬ Go **straight on** along clear track, gradually climbing out of valley back to **4**.
▬ If using ♿, to continue walk read from **4**.
▬ Otherwise, go **right**; retrace steps past Fell End Farm back to Grizedale Head.

WALK 7

CATCH A BUS

SALTERFORTH
AND
BARNOLDSWICK

Salterforth at the start of the walk is a small ex-cotton mill village on the outskirts of the larger Barnoldswick. The walk starts on the towpath of the Leeds and Liverpool Canal by the historic Anchor Inn and eases past the colourful house barges. Barnoldswick has a pleasant town centre, where there's a market square surrounded by cafés and interesting shops. There's a bit of a climb to Letcliffe Park summit but it's always interesting with wonderful pastoral panoramas: Weets Hill on one side and Ingleborough and the hills of Craven on the other.

OS information

🅐 SD 887453
Explorer OL41

Distance
3.75 miles/6km

Time
2½ hours

Start/Finish
Salterforth
Finish for wheelchairs/ pushchairs: Market Square, Barnoldswick

Parking BB18 5TT
Salterforth canalside car park

Public toilets
Kelbrook Road, Salterforth; Fern Lea Avenue car park, Barnoldswick; Letcliffe Park

Cafés/pubs
Anchor Inn, at start; Barnoldswick

Terrain
Canal towpath; pavement; tarred and paved paths and field paths

Hilliness
Steady climb to Letcliffe Park and steady descent to canal

Footwear
Winter 🥾
Spring/Summer/ Autumn 👟

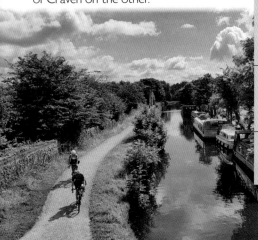

Did you know? The Trent engine, the first ever turbo-propeller aero engine to fly, was designed and developed in Barnoldswick.

Local legend There have been many sightings of phantom Avro Lancaster bombers, which are said to haunt the sky in the Barnoldswick region. In one such case the Craven Herald reported in 2004 that a retired policewoman had seen a large grey aeroplane appear out of the mist near the Rolls Royce factory. It was flying without a sound and really low towards her car and nearby houses, then disappeared without trace.

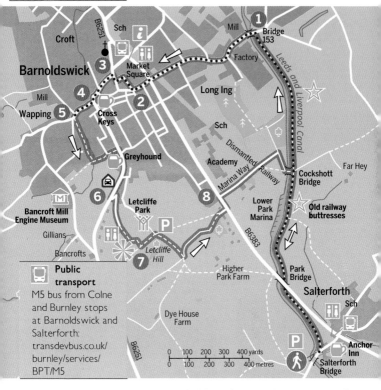

Public transport
M5 bus from Colne and Burnley stops at Barnoldswick and Salterforth: transdevbus.co.uk/burnley/services/BPT/M5

STORIES BEHIND THE WALK

☆ The Growth of a town – early days

There's a reference to Barnoldswick in the Domesday Book under its then name Bernulfesuuic, which means Bernulf's (a Saxon nobleman) settlement. A Cistercian abbey was founded here in 1147 by the Norman baron, Henry de Lacy but was not completed and abandoned in 1152 by the abbot in favour of Kirkstile Abbey, near Leeds.

☆ Rail and Canal

Two things changed Barnoldswick's status as a sleepy village. First, the building of the Leeds–Liverpool Canal in the 1770s, which helped the town become a centre in the cotton industry. This was followed by the Midland Railway's decision to connect it to the Colne–Skipton line at Earby. Industry thrived, including the Rolls Royce aero engine development plant, Esse Stoves, and the Silentnight bed factory. The railway closed in the 1960s – you will see the buttresses of the railway bridge over the canal near Lower Park Marina.

🍵 Anchor Inn ☆ **L e e d s – L i v e r p o o l   C a n a l**

Lower Park Marina   Old railway buttresses

🅿 Salterforth Bridge

1½ mile

🚶 ▪ With your back to the bridge and Anchor Inn leave car park to follow canal towpath for 1 mile, passing under two bridges and by Lower Park Marina to reach Bridge 153.

1 ▪ Ascend ramp to road by Silentnight factory. Turn **left** for ½ mile to town centre.
▪ Go **straight on** at traffic lights and along a row of shops to reach Frank Street on right.

2 ▪ Turn **right** along Frank Street, which leads to the Market Square.
▪ Bend **left** here into Albert Street then **right** along Newtown (one-way) to main road.

❄ Letcliffe Park

Letcliffe Park was developed in the first part of the 20th century. Since 2019 there's been a sculpture trail, developed after the success of the Pendle Sculpture Trail. One of the more interesting features is the bandstand, which is surrounded by low hedges planted to give the effect of a Roman amphitheatre. The park's summit offers wonderful views of the surrounding hills, including Ingleborough, and villages of the valley.

☆ Cotton

The cotton industry was the catalyst for Barnoldswick's growth during the Industrial Revolution. Many mills were opened at this time, including Mitchell's Mill, initially a water mill powered by the stream you pass beside from ⑤. The last mill to be built in Barnoldswick was the Bancroft Mill which ran from 1920 until 1978. Its 600hp steam engine has been preserved in the old engine house, now a museum. It is often in steam and open to the public.

Market Square

☕ Cross Keys

Bridge 153

1½ miles

mile

③ ➡ Turn **left** along Church Street and reach the Cross Keys pub on left.

④ ➡ Just beyond pub fork **right** onto Walmsgate, signed Bancroft Mill Engine.
➡ In 150 yards look for small car park with height barrier on left.

NATURE NOTES

Mute swans can be seen gliding gracefully on the canal, bossing the smaller mallards and coots. A black knob above the orange beak differentiates the mute swan from yellow-beaked Bewick and whooper swans. Mute swans got their name because they are much less vocal than other swans. Their nests are built on huge mounds made from waterside vegetation.

On the canal banks around Lower Park Marina you'll see bulrush, yellow flag iris, and also purple loosestrife, a beautiful moisture-loving perennial plant with spears of showy purple flowers, which can

each grow up to a foot long. The whole plant can be several feet tall.

Grey squirrels can be seen scurrying from tree to tree in Letcliffe Park , where you could also see the small copper butterfly. If you're lucky you may spot a stoat here. Stoats feed mostly on small mammals such as mice and voles, but are voracious and daring predators, capable of catching rabbits that are much larger than themselves. Related to the weasel and otter, the stoat has a long, thin body with sandy brown fur, a white throat and underbelly, with short legs and a long tail.

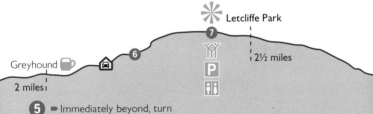

Letcliffe Park

2½ miles

Greyhound

2 miles

5 ➤ Immediately beyond, turn **left** along paved path for 250 yards to path T-junction.
➤ Go **left** and follow path past terraced cottages to Manchester Road by Greyhound pub.
➤ Turn **right** for 275 yards to stone-pillared gateway. (Ignore country park sign up steps – narrow and slippery.)

6 ➤ Rise with stone wall (right) round **right** hairpin bend to Letcliffe Park, passing toilets and playground to reach summit car parks.

Mute swan

Above: purple loosestrife
Left: bulrush
Below: stoat

Leeds–Liverpool Canal ☆

Anchor Inn

3 miles Cockshott Bridge   3½ miles

Salterforth Bridge

7 ➤ Aim for small gate and squeeze stile beyond, over on left boundary, then take **right** fork field path descending to step-stile.

➤ Cross stile and turn **left** along stony track descending to Kelbrook Road. Turn **left** here for 75 yards to junction.

8 ➤ Go **right** along Marina Way, which bends right near its end, back to canal.

➤ Turn **left** over Cockshott Bridge then go **right** onto towpath and follow it back to the start.

Opposite (clockwise):
The Priory Café, Scorton;
Royal Oak Hotel,
Garstang.
This page (clockwise):
The Anchor Inn,
Salterforth; Puddleducks
Tea Rooms, Dunsop
Bridge; Lancashire hotpot;
kiosk at former station,
Halton; Th'Owd Tithe
Barn, Garstang

WALK 8

CATCH A BUS

GARSTANG AND GREENHALGH CASTLE

Garstang is the gateway to the Forest of Bowland, and the smooth outlines of the western hills often dominate the view, especially from the Lancaster Canal. The walk starts on the ever-so-green banks of the River Wyre and goes past the Market Cross and old coaching inns on its way to the canal. You get a bird's-eye view of the Wyre from the aqueduct and there's plenty of wildlife and flora along the towpath. And then there's Greenhalgh Castle; the gaunt ruins give a hint to its violent past.

OS information

🚶 SD 493454
Explorer OL41

Distance
3.1 miles/5km

Time
2 hours

Start/Finish
Garstang

Parking PR3 1EB
High Street car park,
Riverside, Garstang

Public toilets
In car park

Cafés/pubs
Garstang

Terrain
Riverside path,
pavement, field path
and towpath

Hilliness
Level

Footwear
Winter 🥾
Spring/Summer/
Autumn 👟

Public transport

Regular bus routes to/from Preston, Morecambe and Blackpool (services 40-42): stagecoachbus.com/routes/cumbria-and-north-lancashire

Accessibility

Wheelchairs and pushchairs as far as ⑤, with return to Garstang along Bonds Lane

Dogs

Welcome but keep on leads. Three stiles

Did you know? In 1863 a railway line between Garstang and Knott End was proposed. It was heavily supported by local farmers who thought it would enhance the potential of their unproductive mossy land. Money was always scarce and the line only reached Stakepool near Pilling, 4 miles short of Knott End. The line was affectionately known as the Pilling Pig, which referred to the high-pitched squeal of the 0-6-0 *Farmer's Friend* steam engine's whistle. The railway finally closed in 1963.

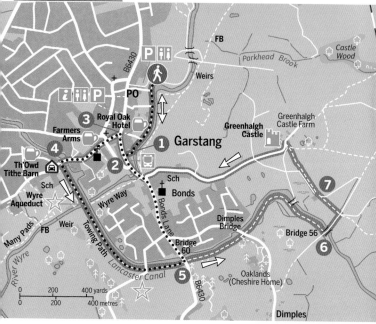

STORIES BEHIND
THE WALK

☆ **Garstang Heritage** Garstang appeared in the Domesday Book as Cherestanc in 1086. The name mutated to Geresteng and later Gayrestang (1292). There has been a market in Garstang since the early 14th century. Held on Thursdays it covers the length of the High Street to the Market Cross, which is surrounded by cobbles. It is thought that the Market Cross lost its cross in the time of Oliver Cromwell, whose troops used the next door Royal Oak pub during the Civil War. Famous visitors to the inn include writer and poet, Sir Walter Scott (1771-1832).

☆ **Garstang Today** The small town built on the banks of the River Wyre is a gateway to Bowland and has many old buildings that have unfortunately been rebuilt in the 19th and 20th centuries. Notable ones you'll see are Th'Owd Tithe Barn, now a canalside pub/restaurant, which used to store the tithes (taxes) collected for the church. The stone-built, two-arched Wyre Bridge dates back to 1492, though the present structure was built in 1629 and later widened.

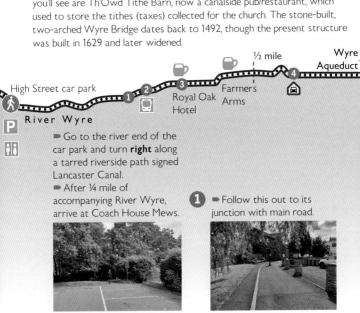

High Street car park

River Wyre

➡ Go to the river end of the car park and turn **right** along a tarred riverside path signed Lancaster Canal.
➡ After ¼ mile of accompanying River Wyre, arrive at Coach House Mews.

Royal Oak Hotel · Farmers Arms · ½ mile · Wyre Aqueduct ☆

1 ➡ Follow this out to its junction with main road.

☆ Canal and Aqueduct

The Lancaster Canal reached Garstang in 1797. The construction included an aqueduct designed by Sir John Rennie. The single-span aqueduct, built from sandstone blocks, is 110 feet long and carries the canal 34 feet above the Wyre. Garstang Basin is an attractive marina overlooked by Th'Owd Tithe Barn restaurant.

Greenhalgh Castle

Thomas Stanley, the 1st Earl of Derby, built Greenhalgh Castle in 1490. The land had been granted to him by Henry VII for helping him defeat Richard III at the Battle of Bosworth Field. The castle had four square castellated towers linked by thick walls that enclosed a rectangular courtyard, all ringed by a circular moat. Garstang was notably Royalist in the Civil War, as was the castle's owner James Stanley, the 7th Earl of Derby. After being under siege the castle's garrison surrendered in 1645 and Cromwell had it destroyed. The ruins of a single tower are all that remains today but there is no permitted access.

1 mile   **5** Bridge 60   1½ miles

☆ L a n c a s t e r   C a n a l

3 ▸ Turn **left** beyond hotel.
▸ At mini-roundabout go **straight on** and pass the Farmers Arms to reach Lancaster Canal.
▸ Cross the canal using the pedestrian section of bridge on right-hand side.

2 ▸ Turn **right** along Bridge Street and enter Market Place by Royal Oak Hotel.

NATURE NOTES

The grey heron is a common visitor to both the Wyre and the canal, where you'll see it patiently waiting for a passing fish. This long-legged wading bird is mainly grey in colour with a white neck and head with a black flash that continues on its crest. Herons can grow to 3 feet tall. Although they feed mainly on fish and frogs, herons can occasionally be seen hunting in fields where they catch small birds and mammals. Their huge nests are made high in the taller trees.

On the canalside you'll see yellow flag iris, reed mace and the yellow water lily. The yellow water lily has cupped bright yellow flowers, much smaller than the cultivated ones you see in garden ponds, and large leathery oval leaves on the surface with smaller more rounded submerged leaves. This perennial blooms between June and September. The lily's flowers are pollinated by flies and beetles and its leaves provide food and shelter for fish, snails and many underwater insects.

☆ Lancaster Canal

⑥ Bridge 56　⑦ ¦ 2 miles

Greenhalgh Castle

Greenhalgh Farm

④ ➟ Once over the canal, **cross** road and go **straight ahead** onto the canal towpath.
➟ **Keep forward** to pass over the Wyre Aqueduct in 250 yards.
➟ In another ½ mile reach Bridge 60.

⑤ ➟ Wheelchairs and pushchairs should leave canal here to avoid stiles later in walk: cross bridge and follow Bonds Lane to cross River Wyre then take second exit at roundabout to retrace steps from ⑦.
➟ Otherwise **continue** along towpath to Bridge 56.

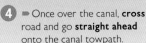

Throughout May and June you'll see cow parsley, a tall plant with flat umbrellas of small white flowers and fern-like leaves. Cow parsley likes shady places such as roadside verges beneath hedgerows and the perimeters of woodland. It is widespread on this walk and can be seen on the edges of fields and along the canal banks. It attracts many creatures, including orange-tip butterflies, hoverflies and rabbits.

Top: cow parsley
Left: grey heron
Opposite page
Left: yellow water lily
Right: orange-tip butterfly

2½ miles

Coach House Mews

River Wyre

3 miles

High Street car park

7 ▬ Go through yard and leave track at bend to follow waymarker arrow across field. Over two more stiles the path comes to the Greenhalgh Castle Farm complex.

▬ Turn **left** along lane for ½ mile to main road. Go **right** and take second exit at roundabout back to **2**. Retrace steps by the river to car park.

6 ▬ Climb steps to top of bridge then turn **left** over short section of rough grassy track.

▬ Go through farm gate then turn **left** over stile in hedge.

▬ Head across fields towards farm outbuildings in 200 yards.

WALK 9

BEACON FELL

It's only 872 feet above sea level but Beacon Fell offers pleasing, ever-changing views to the Bowland moors, fells and pikes. These give way to the flat fields of the Fylde, the West Pennine Moors and Morecambe Bay. On a clear day you might even spot the Isle of Man.

The country park is popular so arrive early at peak times. There is a lovely mix of conifer and broad-leaved woodland and, while the highlight might well be a large snake or maybe a love seat, there's always something interesting to see.

OS information

⊕ SD 578421
Explorer OL41

Distance
2.5 miles/4km

Time
1½ hours

Start/Finish
Beacon Fell Country Park

Parking PR3 2NJ
Carwags Picnic Area car park, Carwags Lane.
♿ **for wheelchairs and pushchairs**: PR3 2EW The Mosses car park, Beacon Fell Road

Public toilets
Carwags Picnic Area; Beacon Fell Visitor Centre

Cafés/pubs
Café at Beacon Fell Visitor Centre

Terrain
Mostly good paths and tracks

Hilliness
Moderately undulating hillslopes

Footwear
Winter 🥾
Spring/Summer/
Autumn 👟

🚌 **Public
transport**
None

♿ **Accessibility**
▪▪▪▪▪▪▪▪▪▪▪

The circuit beginning/
ending at ♿
is suitable for
wheelchairs and
pushchairs

🐕 **Dogs**
Welcome. No
stiles

Did you know? German airmen from World
War II used Fell House Farm, which stood
on the current site of the visitor centre, as a
navigational marker for their raids on Liverpool
and Manchester.

Local legend Chingle Hall is a gaunt mansion
south of nearby Goosnargh, built in 1260 by
Norman baron, Adam de Singleton, with a moat
and drawbridge. Descendants also added priest
holes to hide Catholic clergy from persecution
during the 16th-century Reformation. The hall
is thought to be one of England's most haunted
houses. Some people say monks from the past
still haunt the site while others think they've
seen the ghost of Lady Eleanor de Singleton, the
last of that family to own the estate.

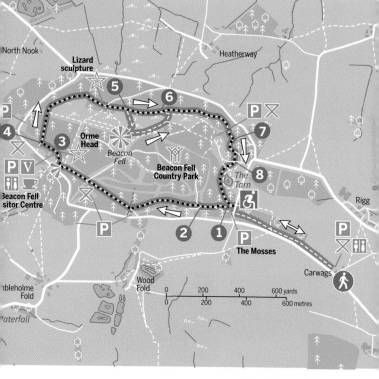

STORIES BEHIND THE WALK

☆ **Beacon Fell – past and present** The fell had for centuries been used as farmland pasture, but in 1909 Fulwood Urban District Council acquired it for its water supply. The water was collected in the Barnsfold reservoirs to the south-east, where it was distributed by pipeline. At the time the fell was afforested with conifers to help with drainage. The scheme was ended in 1959 and the reservoirs are now used for angling. Lancashire Country Council bought the site in 1969 and opened it as a country park in 1970. They built a one-way circular road around the perimeter to ease the flow of traffic, added several car parks and built a visitor centre on the site of Fell House Farm.

The Mosses car park 🅿 ♿

1
½ mile

Carwags car park

🅿
🚻
✕

➡ A narrow path, parallel to (but avoiding) lane, leaves car park and comes to Beacon Fell Road in ⅓ mile.
➡ Turn **right** and shortly go **left** into the Mosses car park ♿.

1 ➡ Follow the wide track at the back of the car park for about 200 yards to track junction.

2 ➡ Fork **left**, signed to visitor centre. Descend through larch woods.
➡ Where a path comes in on left from road, veer **right**, uphill.
➡ Ignoring side paths, **keep forward** for ¼ mile to reach sloping green above visitor centre.

☆ **Historic Beacons** Beacons on high hills have been used for over a thousand years. The fires were lit to convey messages or warnings of imminent danger. Beacon Hill's isolation and visibility from the surrounding countryside made it an ideal site and there are records as far back as 1002 of one being lit here. The fell would have been part of the chain to warn of the approach of the Spanish Armada in 1588, also the French troops in the late 18th and early 19th centuries. They have also been used in celebration of royal events.

☆ **Wooden sculptures** The work of Thompson Dagnall is featured in the park's sculpture trail. Above the visitor centre you'll see the *Orme Head* stone, a rather grotesque carving of a squinting face; and in the forest a magnificent huge basking snake is among the exhibits, which also include an owl wood carving, a lizard 'seat' and a dragonfly. They are all dotted around the park, waiting for you to discover them.

☆ Beacon Fell Visitor Centre

✕ ☕ 🛉 P V

⊢ 1 mile

3 ➡ Aim for the *Orme Head* sculpture and leave visitor centre on stony path that climbs steadily across the fellside to path junction in 150 yards.

4 ➡ Turn **right** with the wide path. This climbs initially then curves right, gradually rising on north side of fell.
➡ Go straight on at lizard seat sculpture intersection to junction in 100 yards.

NATURE NOTES

The woods of Beacon Fell were at one time mainly conifer, such as Sitka spruce, Scots pine and European larch, but these are gradually being replaced with native broad-leaved trees such as oak, rowan and silver birch.

There are twelve types of dragonfly and damselfly in the park and you're likely to see them at The Tarn near **8**. Among the species here are southern and common hawker dragonflies and blue-tailed and large red damselflies. They lay their eggs which, a few weeks later, will hatch into nymphs that will live in the pond for up to five years. The nymphs are aggressive predators and can even be a danger to small fish.

When they emerge the damselflies are lighter-bodied than dragonflies and fold their wings when at rest – dragonflies hold their wings flat.

Skylarks and meadow pipits are seen in the open areas near the summit of the fell. In the Mosses area you may see lapwing and curlew. Snipe are also found here, for the wet environment is aided by a rainwater drainage pipe further up the hill. This medium-sized wading bird with a wingspan of about 15 inches has brown and fawn back feathers, a mottled brown and fawn chest, shortish legs and a long flexible beak which it uses to probe mud for worms.

1½ miles

5 Lizard sculpture

Beacon Fell (Detour to summit)

6 Beacon Fell (Detour returns to main path)

7

5 ➡ Main route continues for 200 yards to next junction.
➡ Optionally (not suitable for wheelchairs and pushchairs), for summit viewpoint detour, go **right** and climb to trig point. There, turn **left** to rejoin main route at **6**, but just before reaching it go sharp **left** to do so (ignore red route, right).

6 ➡ For non-summiteers, fork **left**; summiteers turn sharp **right**.
➡ Walk for a ¼ mile, ignoring a right-hand side path, to a waymarked T-junction in woodland.

Common hawker dragonfly

Top: skylark
Middle: rowan berries
Bottom: snipe

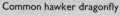

The Tarn

8

2 miles

P ♿ The Mosses
car park

Carwags
car park

2½ miles

P

🚻

✕

8 ⇒ Cross over to pass to **right** of The Tarn (dragonfly pond). The path comes to the outward track near **1**.
⇒ Turn **left** to the Mosses car park. To continue to Carwags, turn **right** onto lane and then **left** along narrow path.

7 ⇒ Turn **right** and then **right** again near a car park to arrive at a lane.

EDISFORD BRIDGE AND THE RIVER RIBBLE

After a visit to historic Clitheroe and its castle, a stroll along the River Ribble from Edisford Bridge is a must. The picnic area around the bridge is a lovely place to start. There's a little railway and playgrounds for the children too. The walk is easy paced and pleasant in its entirety and at the halfway point the Aspinall Arms offers refreshment. After a short roadside stretch, the return route traverses fields, follows a section of a Roman road, then rejoins the Ribble back to the start.

OS information

SD 727413
Explorer OL41

Distance
5.3 miles/8.5km

Time
3½ hours

Start/Finish
Edisford Bridge, Clitheroe

Parking BB7 2FE
Edisford Road car park

Public toilets
In car park

Cafés/pubs
Kiosk by Edisford Bridge; pubs: Edisford Bridge; Aspinall Arms, Great Mitton

Terrain
Roads; mostly good riverside and field paths, and tracks

Hilliness
Mostly level

Footwear
Winter 🥾
Spring/Summer/ Autumn 👟

Public transport
Train services to Clitheroe. No 2 bus from Clitheroe centre to nearby Low Moor, just east of 🚶 along Edisford Road: bustimes.org/ services/2-clitheroe-low-moor-circular-via-henthorn

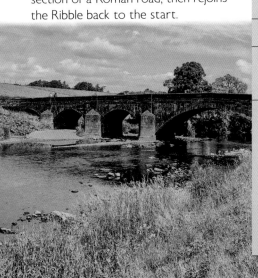

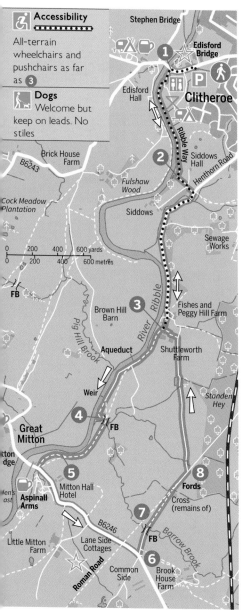

Accessibility
▪▪▪▪▪▪▪▪▪▪▪
All-terrain wheelchairs and pushchairs as far as ③

Dogs
Welcome but keep on leads. No stiles

Did you know? After a meeting held in Clitheroe's Swan and Royal Hotel in 1942, Rolls Royce took over the development of Sir Frank Whittle's jet engine from the Rover company.

Local legend Waddow Hall is a grand 17th-century mansion overlooking the Ribble's banks north-west of Clitheroe. The hall is said to be haunted by the ghost of Peg o' Nell, known as Peg o' th'Well. Legend has it that Peg, a servant of the hall, was so evil that she drove her mistress to distraction. The mistress is said to have murdered Peg, either by pushing her into a well, or by the blow of an axe. But Peg was vengeful and, according to folklore, her spirit has claimed several lives in the river, including that of a Puritan teacher who drowned trying to cross on the nearby stepping stones.

STORIES BEHIND THE WALK

☆ **Edisford Bridge** The River Ribble here is quite wide but shallow, allowing it to be forded easily, hence the name Edisford. It was an important crossing and the site of the Battle of Clitheroe in 1138, part of a civil war known as the Anarchy. The claim to King Stephen's throne had been disputed by the Empress Matilda. Helped by forces loyal to King David I of Scotland, the empress won the battle; but King Stephen eventually won the war.

A sandstone bridge was built here in 1339 but it has been much modified and widened over the centuries.

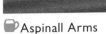

🍵**Aspinall Arms**
The 17th-century Aspinall Arms was at one time known as the Mitton Boat. Before the bridge over the Ribble was constructed in the 19th century, travellers were ferried across the water in a rowing boat.

☆ Edisford Bridge

P ✕
Edisford Road
car park

① ½ mile

② ‖1 mile

Henthorn Road

➊ ➡ Turn **left** just before bridge on path across a green, down towards the river.
➡ Follow path (Ribble Way) past a refreshment kiosk and **continue** by river to where it turns left through a gate.

➋ ➡ Follow stony track to reach lane. Turn **right** along this for over ½ mile to Fishes and Peggy Hill Farm, and **continue** another 100 yards to Shuttleworth Farm.

➡ From the far end of car park use pedestrian exit and turn **left** on pavement down to Edisford Bridge.

☆ Clitheroe's history

The name Clitheroe is derived from the Anglo-Saxon word meaning rocky hill, and the settlement dates back to that time. After the Norman invasion the land was given to Roger de Poitou. It was passed on to the powerful de Lacy family and, in 1186, Robert de Lacy built the castle on that rocky hill. The three-storey stone-built keep is said to be the second smallest in England. It later became the property of the Duchy of Lancaster. The keep suffered damage in the English Civil War and lost its roof. Within the grounds are beautiful gardens and a museum, which is situated in the 18th-century Castle House.

☆ Roman Road

Some of the return route follows the line of an old Roman road, Margary 72a, that linked forts at Ribchester and York via Downham under Pendle Hill. The road would have probably been paved with stone, metalled and cambered for drainage, aided by ditches alongside the main carriageway. This was a major road for centuries after the Romans left and yet Clitheroe and many other towns were built slightly away from it. This was to avoid invaders and robbers who might be halting wealthy travellers or stealing drovers' cattle.

uttleworth rm

River Ribble

Aqueduct pipe

Weir

½ miles

④

2 miles

⑤

Aspinall Arms

Mitton Hall

Mitton Road

2½ miles

③ ➡ Just before farm buildings, fork **right** through kissing-gate across small field then out through another to pass **right** of farmhouse.
➡ Follow stony riverside track beyond, passing a pipeline aqueduct then a weir.

④ ➡ 175 yards beyond weir, bend **left** with path then cross **right** over footbridge. A gated path continues across fields.
➡ Continue parallel to tree-lined river until Aspinall Arms comes into view.

NATURE NOTES

You'll see coots, mallards and mute swans by Edisford Bridge. Otters are on the increase along the River Ribble. This large member of the weasel family is brown in colour and has a slender body with a powerful neck, a long, flattened tail and webbed feet, which make it a strong and agile swimmer. The otter feeds largely on fish supplemented by frogs and the occasional small riverside mammal.

The noisy oystercatcher is a common sight over the River Ribble. This black and white wader has a red beak and long red legs. It feeds on worms and insect larvae. Like the cuckoo, the oystercatcher will sometimes lay its eggs in another bird's nest.

The dog rose can be seen on this walk in the hedgerows among the hawthorns and beech. It is a thorny climbing rose which clasps onto other plants with its curved spines. It can grow up to 10 feet high in the right conditions and has beautiful pink or white five-petalled flowers. On pollination the rose produces red, oval, berry-like hips containing hairy seeds.

Roman Road ☆

6 Lane Side Cottages

7 Footbridge
3 miles

8 Cross (remains of)

3½ miles

Shuttleworth Farm

4 mile

5 ➡ At this point, stay close to right-hand field edge. Pass **left** of pub and turn **left** along roadside pavement.
➡ **Keep forward** for ½ mile past Mitton Hall to road bend after Lane Side Cottages.

6 ➡ Go through the walkers' gate and through the trees, taking the **left** fork path to reach gated-footbridge.

Top left: otter
Top right: oystercatcher
Above: dog rose
Left: coot
Opposite: mallard

Edisford
Bridge

iver Ribble   ¦ 4½ miles   5 miles   Edisford Road
                                             car park

7 ▰ Over bridge follow left-hand field edge and cross another footbridge.
▰ In 300 yards keep eyes peeled for a field path junction near the base of an ancient cross.

8 ▰ Take the faint **left** fork towards the trees and hedge.
▰ Go through kissing-gate and follow hedge on right. Back at Shuttleworth Farm turn **left** through farmyard to **3**.
▰ Retrace outward route back to car park.

Ordnance Survey

Publishing information

© Crown copyright 2023.
All rights reserved.

Ordnance Survey, OS, and the OS logos are registered trademarks, and OS Short Walks Made Easy is a trademark of Ordnance Survey Ltd.

© Crown copyright and database rights (2023) Ordnance Survey.

ISBN 978 0 319092 60 6
1st edition published by Ordnance Survey 2023.

www.ordnancesurvey.co.uk

While every care has been taken to ensure the accuracy of the route directions, the publishers cannot accept responsibility for errors or omissions, or for changes in details given. The countryside is not static: hedges and fences can be removed, stiles can be replaced by gates, field boundaries can alter, footpaths can be rerouted and changes in ownership can result in the closure or diversion of some concessionary paths. Also, paths that are easy and pleasant for walking in fine conditions may become slippery, muddy and difficult in wet weather.

If you find an inaccuracy in either the text or maps, please contact Ordnance Survey at os.uk/contact.

A catalogue record for this book is available from the British Library.

Milestone Publishing credits

Author: John Gillham

Series editor: Kevin Freeborn

Maps: Cosmographics

Design and Production: Patrick Dawson, Milestone Publishing

Printed in India by Replika Press Pvt. Ltd

MIX
Paper from responsible sources
FSC
www.fsc.org   FSC® C016779

Photography credits

Front cover: ©John Gillham. **Back cover** cornfield/Shutterstock.com.

All photographs supplied by the author ©John Gillham except page 6 Rory Southworth; 66 Kevin Freeborn.

The following images were supplied by Shutterstock.com: pages 1 TravellingFatman; 6 Honour Burges Photography; 6 AlanMorris; 8 DMC Photogallery; 18 LifeisticAC; 19 novama; 19, 41, 79 Rudmer Zwerver; 25 Roel Meijer; 25 RudiErnst; 25 Tatyana Mi; 26 Brenda Kean; 26 Paxels; 29 jim cooke; 31 Debra O'Connor; 33 Andrew M. Allport; 33 Glenn Price; 33 JLund; 33 Jorge Macedo; 33 Ondrej Prosicky; 35 Chris Waistle; 39 jamie corney; 39 Paul Aniszewski; 39 soohyun kim; 40 Marek Mierzejewski; 40 Richard P Long; 40 Vlad Sokolovsky; 41 Ian Fletcher; 41 ranchorunner; 41 Wang LiQiang; 45 Anne Coatesy; 47 alitellioglu; 47 thatmacroguy; 52 Sandra Standbridge; 53 Anastasiia Malinich; 53 Leo Bucher; 53 Safargalieva Ilsiar; 59 Stephan Morris; 59 Stephen Whybrow; 60 Fencewood Studios; 60 istetiana; 73 fasenda; 73 FotoRequest; 73 Rob Christiaans; 77 Matt_Turner; 79 Steve Midgley; 79 Wayne Tuckwell.

The following images were supplied via Wikimedia Commons: pages 17 Burtonsi, CC BY-SA 4.0; 45 Alexander P Kapp, CC BY-SA 2.0; 63 Ian Taylor, CC BY-SA 2.0; 73 Tony Hisgett CC BY-SA 2.0.